DECADES OF THE
20TH
CENTURY

1930s

ELDORADO INK

DECADES OF THE 20TH CENTURY

1900s

1910s

1920s

1930s

1940s

1950s

1960s

1970s

1980s

1990s

DECADES OF THE 20TH CENTURY

1930s

ELDORADO INK

Published by Eldorado Ink
2099 Lost Oak Trail
Prescott, AZ 86303
www.eldoradoink.com

Copyright © 2005 Rebo International b.v., Lisse

Milan Bobek, Editor
Judith C. Callomon, Historical consultant
Samuel J. Patti, Consulting editor

Printed and bound in Slovenia

Publisher Cataloging Data
1930s / [Milan Bobek, editor].
        p. cm. -- (Decades of the 20th century)
        Includes index.
        Summary: This volume, arranged chronologically, presents key events that have shaped the decade, from significant political occurrences to details of daily life.
        ISBN 1-932904-03-4
        1. Nineteen thirties   2. History, Modern--20th century--Chronology   3. History, Modern--20th century--Pictorial works
  I. Bobek, Milan   II. Title: Nineteen thirties   III. Series
        909.82/3--dc22

Picture research and photography by Anne Hobart Lang and Rolf Lang of AHL Archives. Additional research by Heritage Picture Collection, London.

CONTENTS

THE GREAT DEPRESSION

A frightening decade of extreme ideologies, economic disaster, and war. Communism, Fascism, and Nazism confront each other, each led by fanatical leaders. Adolf Hitler's image, stage-managed rallies, and swastika sign dominate these ten years. Gandhi takes the opposite path, by advocating nonviolent resistance. Financial depression leads to global poverty. In the United States, Roosevelt introduces the New Deal while in China, Mao Zedong leads the Long March. Nothing can stop the inevitability of World War II, which brings the decade to an end.

OPPOSITE: Adolf Hitler and his followers at one of the many Nazi rallies of the decade.

1930–1939

KEY EVENTS OF THE DECADE

- CIVIL WAR IN CHINA
- THE RISE OF STALIN
- GANDHI AND CIVIL DISOBEDIENCE
- AIRSHIP DISASTERS
- NAZISM IN ASCENDANCY
- THE CULT OF HITLER
- PLASTIC AND NYLON
- JET AIRCRAFT
- SPANISH CIVIL WAR
- RADIO FROM SPACE

- FINANCIAL DEPRESSION
- THE NEW DEAL
- THE LONG MARCH
- THE OKLAHOMA DUST BOWL
- WAR BETWEEN ITALY AND ETHIOPIA
- KEYNESIAN ECONOMIC THEORY
- WORLD WAR II BEGINS
- REPEAL OF PROHIBITION

WORLD POPULATION: 2,070 MILLION

PLASTICS, PLUTO, AND THE RISE OF NAZISM

The new decade brings civil war in China and revolt in India as Gandhi shows civil disobedience to the British. The new material, plastic, is met with enthusiasm by designers working in the new art deco style. Haile Selassie is crowned emperor of Ethiopia and in Germany, the jackboot stamps into the Reichstag as Hitler's Nazi Party proves to be a vote winner. In France, André Maginot takes the threat of German expansionism to heart and begins constructing the defensive Maginot Line. Triumph is in the air. Amy Johnson is the first woman to fly from Europe to Australia and the prototype jet engine is patented. A new planet swims into view: Pluto, named after the god of the underworld.

1930

Feb	**18**	American astronomer Clyde Tombaugh discovers the planet Pluto
Apr	**6**	Gandhi and his followers end their march to the sea in protest against the salt laws imposed by the British in India
	24	Amy Johnson lands in Australia after flying from Britain
July	**1**	In the United States, the first Greyhound bus pulls out of the garage
Nov	**2**	Haile Selassie is crowned emperor of Ethiopia

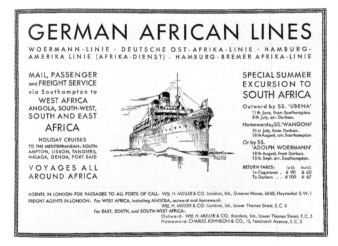

ABOVE: Europe and the great African continent are linked by fast, regular mail steamers offering every modern comfort and convenience for their passengers.

OPPOSITE: The British airship, the *R101*, crashes into a French hillside on its maiden voyage.

CIVIL WAR IN CHINA

This year sees the start of the war fought between the Kuomintang (KMT) Nationalist armies of Chiang Kai-shek and the Communists, which is to last until 1934. The KMT drive the Communists out of their bases in the southern mountains of China and force them on the Long March to new bases. Mao Zedong is among the marchers.

COLLECTIVIZE OR DIE

Following the success of the Five Year Plan in collectivizing all smallholdings, Stalin extends the program to larger farms, ordering the kulaks, or rich peasants, to hand over their land. Millions of kulaks are subsequently killed as collectivization is ruthlessly enforced.

THE SALT MARCH

In India, Gandhi begins a campaign of civil disobedience against British rule by protesting the government monopoly of salt production. He leads a march to the sea, to make a symbolic amount of salt from sea water. His arrest and imprisonment in April causes widespread rioting and strikes across India.

FIRST CYCLOTRON

An American team led by Ernest O. Lawrence builds the world's first experimental cyclotron, a device that accelerates atomic particles in a circle.

ABOVE: Children in a Russian collective are cared for in a kindergarten so that their mothers can work on the land. This was part of Stalin's first Five Year Plan for the collectivization and industrialization of agriculture.

FIRST WORLD CUP

Only 13 nations, of which just four are from Europe, compete in the first football World Cup in Uruguay on July 30. The United States is one of four seeded nations. The hosts win, beating neighboring Argentina 4–2, starting a trend of victories by host nations. The competition is the brainchild of Frenchman Guerin and Dutchman Hirschman.

FLYING SOUTH

English pilot Amy Johnson (1903–1941) arrives in Australia in her Gipsy Moth on May 24. She is the first woman to make a long distance solo flight from London. She sets a world record of six days from London to India and reaches Darwin in 19 days.

HAILE SELASSIE

In April, Ras Tafari, regent of Ethiopia, becomes emperor on the death of the empress. He takes the name Haile Selassie and will be crowned in November. Rastafarians in Jamaica, British West Indies, hail him as a living god, the fulfillment of a prophecy by American black nationalist leader Marcus Garvey.

PLUTO DISCOVERED

American astronomer Clyde W. Tombaugh, working at the Lowell Observatory in the United States, discovers Pluto, the outermost planet. Its existence has been predicted by Percival Lowell. It proves to have an irregular orbit around the Sun.

WHITE VOTES IN SOUTH AFRICA

In May, white South African women win the vote, but black men and women remain disenfranchised.

EXTREMISM COMES TO POWER

The Nazis make huge advances in the general election in September, gaining 107 seats, second only to the Socialists. The growing economic crisis in Germany, after the Wall Street Crash, causes many to support the party in the hope that it can provide a strong government for Germany.

FIRST LARGE COMPUTER

A team led by American scientist Vannevar Bush develops the world's first big analogue computer, an electromechanical machine.

FANTASTIC PLASTIC

Solid, clear plastics are made from acrylic acid discovered by scientists in Britain, Canada, and Germany in the 1920s. They will go on the market as Perspex in Britain and as Lucite and Plexiglas in North America.

ABOVE: Mahatma Gandhi, marked by an arrow in the picture, watching as his followers scoop up sand and salt water at Dandi, defying the government.

ABOVE: Amy Johnson, in her Gipsy Moth *Jason*, becomes the first woman to fly solo from England to Australia. A year later, she will make a recordbreaking solo flight to Cape Town.

ABOVE: Adolf Hitler inspires the party faithful at a vast open-air rally held to celebrate the recent election success of the National Socialists (Nazis).

ABOVE: Plastic frames for glasses encasing lace and other fabrics become a fashionable designer accessory as makers experiment with this new acrylic material.

ART DECO REACHES NEW HEIGHTS

The Chrysler Building in New York, designed by William van Alen, is completed. Phantasmagoric art deco detailing (the steel-faced, seven story spire, the curving lines of the top stories, the interior decoration, the doorways) make this perhaps the most beautiful of all skyscrapers. Until the Empire State Building is completed, it will remain the highest building in the world at 1,056 feet.

THE BEST THING SINCE ...

Sliced bread is introduced in the United States under the Wonder Bread label by Continental Baking and the first successful automatic electric toaster is produced by the McGraw-Electric Co. of Elgin, Illinois.

BRIDGES IN SWITZERLAND

Swiss engineer Robert Maillart creates a series of elegant bridges in reinforced concrete, of which the Salginatobel Bridge, with its fine lines and dramatic gorge setting, is the most striking. Functional simplicity produces beauty in Maillart's work.

AMERICAN GOTHIC

This memorable painting of a Midwestern farmer and his wife seems to sum up rural America and becomes a lasting symbol of the rural way of life. Painted in Iowa by Grant Wood (1892–1942), it becomes the most famous painting of the American regionalist group of artists which includes Thomas Hart Benton and John Steuart Curry.

THE FIRST JET ENGINE

British aeroengineer Frank Whittle (1907–1996) patents a jet engine for aircraft use.

BOBBY JONES RETIRES

Bobby Jones retires this year after winning golf's grand slam which consists of the United States and British Opens and the United States and British Amateurs.

FRIDTJOF NANSEN
(1861–1930)

The Norwegian explorer, zoologist, and oceanographer has died. His first Arctic adventure was in 1882 on board a sealer and from 1893 to 1895 he tested his theory that he could reach the North Pole by drifting with an ice floe. He went further north by this method (86°14′N) than anyone had previously. After independence (1905), Nansen was Norwegian ambassador in London (1906-1908). He was the League of Nations commissioner for refugees from 1920-1922, devising the Nansen passport for stateless persons, and won the Nobel Peace Prize in 1922 for his Russian relief work.

TREE SICKNESS

Dutch elm disease, first seen in Holland in 1919, spreads to the United States and attacks American trees.

MIND MATTERS

Karl Menninger, who in 1920 founded with his father the pioneering Menninger psychiatric clinic in Kansas, publishes *The Human Mind*. Although written for medical students, it is widely read because it explains how psychiatry can help mentally disturbed people.

HAYS RULES

The Motion Picture Production Code is established in response to calls for censorship of motion pictures. It is spearheaded by Will H. Hays, president of the Motion Pictures Producers and Distributors (known as the Hays Office). The code consists of a detailed list of what is and is not acceptable on screen.

FRENCH DEFENSE

French workmen begin building the Maginot Line, named after French war minister André Maginot. It is a series of forts built to protect France against possible German invasion.

COUP IN PERU

After an army coup in August, Colonel Luis Sánchez Cerro becomes president of Peru, overthrowing the elected government. A month later, an army revolt in Argentina overthrows the reformist president, Hipólito Irigoyen, and installs a military government under General José Uriburu.

TICKET TO RIDE

The Greyhound Bus Company opens up bus routes all over the United States.

RIGHT: The two spans of the Sydney Harbor Bridge inch towards each other to form the world's largest arch bridge. It will enable pedestrians and road and rail passengers to cross 170 feet above even the largest of the harbor's ocean liners.

WAR IN THE EAST, BUILDING IN THE WEST

Japan flexes its imperial muscle and takes Manchuria from China, initiating the Sino-Japanese War, which will last until 1945. In Spain, a republic is declared, but this will not prevent eventual civil war. In America, despite the Depression, building is on the increase and towers begin to scrape the sky. In France, Swiss architect Charles Jeanneret, better known as Le Corbusier, establishes the canon of modern architectural orthodoxy. Conquering the skies is still very much on the agenda when Swiss scientist Auguste Piccard reaches the stratosphere in a balloon. The disputed father of the light bulb, Thomas Alva Edison, dies.

1931

Feb	5	British racer Malcolm Campbell sets a new world land speed record at Daytona: 245 miles per hour
Mar	3	"The Star-Spangled Banner" becomes the official national anthem of the United States
Apr	14	Spain becomes a republic
May	1	The Empire State Building opens in New York City
	28	Swiss scientist Auguste Piccard balloons to the stratosphere
Oct	24	Al Capone sentenced for tax crime

ABOVE: Robert Frost (1874–1963) wins the Pulitzer Prize for the second time this year. He is one of America's most popular poets.

BIRTH OF THE SPANISH REPUBLIC

King Alfonso abdicates in April and goes into exile in London as Spain is declared a republic. The collapse of the monarchy follows gains made by the Republican party in the local elections. The new government is headed by Alcalá Zamora. In the general election in June, the Socialists make huge gains.

AUSTRIA TRIGGERS EUROPEAN RUIN

In May, the collapse of Credit-Anstalt, a minor Austrian bank, leads to major financial crises throughout Central and Eastern Europe. The crisis spreads to Germany in July and to Britain in August, causing the minority Labour government to fall and a National government, under the leadership of the Labour prime minister, Ramsay MacDonald, to take office. Britain comes off the gold standard and devalues the pound in September, causing financial turmoil around the world. Unemployment soars across Europe.

A COMMONWEALTH CHARTER

The British Parliament passes the Statute of Westminster, which defines the independence of the five dominions within the British Empire. The statute becomes the basic charter of the modern British Commonwealth as British colonies gain their independence.

NIGHT FLIGHT

French writer and aviator Antoine de Saint-Exupéry (1900–1944), author of the well-known children's book, *The Little Prince* (1943), publishes *Night Flight*. It is probably his best book and it details a new South American airline and its chief pilot. The book, which draws on his experiences as a pilot, contributes to the 1930s literary love affair with everything to do with the air and aviation.

EMPIRE STATE BUILDING

The latest of New York's skyscrapers is now the world's tallest building. It is famous for its great height of 1,250 feet (later increased by antennae to 1,472 feet), for the speed of construction, for its shimmering walls (many clad in metal alloy), and its fine foyer. It opens during the Depression and much of the office space remains unlet, but the owners reap revenue from sightseers.

MAIGRET STONEWALLED

Belgian writer Georges Simenon (1903–1989) creates Inspector Jules Maigret in this novel (originally titled *M. Gallet décédé*) and elevates the *roman policier* to a psychological novel of some subtlety. Maigret is notable for being perhaps the first of the "caring" policemen in fiction, a man who solves crimes by understanding the criminals. The books are also famous for their depictions of the atmosphere and even the smells (Simenon had an extraordinary nose) of Paris.

ABOVE: New York City's George Washington Bridge, opened on October 24, spans a recordbreaking 3,609 feet.

ANNA PAVLOVA
(1885–1931)

The Russian ballerina has died. She left Russia in 1909 to work with Diaghilev's Paris-based Ballets Russes. She later set up her own company, becoming internationally known for performing highlights from the classic ballets, perhaps the most celebrated being the dying swan. Pavlova cake is named in her honor.

VILLA SAVOIE

This house at Poissy, France, is one of the most famous by Swiss architect Le Corbusier, and is the physical manifestation of his famous *Five Points of Architecture*. It popularizes the use of concrete pillars (or *pilotis* as Le Corbusier calls them) to raise the living floor above the ground. Other typical features include ribbon windows, white walls, a flat roof, and large terraces.

THE WAVES

English novelist Virginia Woolf (1882–1941) publishes her most experimental work. In it, she describes the lives of a group of friends, from childhood to middle age, through their own words and thoughts. Between the character's thoughts come poetic mood-setting passages describing a seascape, the rising and setting sun, the shore, and the breaking waves.

FRANKENSTEIN'S MONSTER COMES TO LIFE

English-born actor Boris Karloff (1887–1969) stars as the monster in *Frankenstein*, directed by James Whale. It is a film loosely based on Mary Shelley's novel of 1818. This is the most popular of many films based on the story.

PIECE FOR PERCUSSION

French modernist composer Edgard Varèse (1885–1965) writes the first piece of Western music solely for percussion. The piece relies on the contrast between the deep, rich sound of the tam-tam and the drier sound of the military drum.

POPULATION CONTROL

Contraception is forbidden to Roman Catholics by Pope Pius XII in his encyclical Casti Connubi, but approved for Anglicans by the Archbishop of Canterbury. As the world population approaches two billion, abortion is outlawed in Italy by Mussolini.

UP UP AND AWAY

Auguste Piccard (1884–1962), a Swiss physicist, and Charles Kipfew, his assistant, become the first people to reach the stratosphere. They ascend to 55,000 feet in an enclosed, pressurized aluminum sphere carried by a balloon.

KNOW YOUR MARKET

The Starch Ratings are introduced by Daniel Starch, director of the American Association of Advertising Agencies, to measure advertising readership and radio audiences.

FLASH BANG

Electronic flashguns for photographers are invented. This does away with expendable flashbulbs.

LEFT: Smog-bound Pittsburgh (top) gags for control on air pollution, and sighs with relief at the result (bottom).

THOMAS ALVA EDISON
(1847–1931)

The Ohio-born inventor has died. He took out over 1,000 patents during his prolifically industrious life. His inventions range from a vote recording machine and the stock exchange ticker tape, to the phonograph, the incandescent electric light bulb, the humble megaphone, the first electricity power plant, and the "talking" movies.

BRIGHT LIGHTS, BIG CITY?
The first study of air pollution is carried out by the U.S. Public Health Service. It estimates that one-fifth of the natural light of New York City is cut out by smoke pollution.

FASTER SHAVES
The electric razor, patented in 1923 by Colonel Jacob Schick, is produced and marketed by his own company, Schick Dry Shaver, Inc.

RADIO FROM SPACE
U.S. radio engineer Karl G. Jansky discovers radio waves emanating from outside the solar system. This discovery marks the beginning of radio astronomy.

SAFETY KETTLE
British manufacturer Walter Bulpitt invents an electric kettle that automatically ejects a resettable safety plug if the kettle overheats.

ENTER TELEX AND TWX
The American Telephone and Telegraph Company introduces two-way teleprinter services, called TWX in America and Telex in Britain. It can be used by subscribers in their own offices.

THE MORNING AFTER
Alka Seltzer, a new painkiller produced as a tablet that effervesces when dissolved in water, is introduced by Miles Laboratories of Indiana. It contains an antacid indigestion agent and is a popular treatment for hangovers.

SUSPENSION RECORD
The George Washington Bridge over the Hudson River, connecting New York City with New Jersey, is opened. Its suspension span is 3,609 feet, which is a record for the time.

ELECTRON MICROSCOPE
German scientists Ernst Ruska and Max Knoll construct the first electron microscope, which gives a much greater enlargement than ordinary microscopes.

ABOVE: Thomas A. Edison dies. Physicist and world famous inventor, he is shown outside the office of a mining plant seeking his famous "one percent inspiration."

DAME NELLY MELBA (HELEN PORTER ARMSTRONG, née MITCHELL)
(1861–1931)

The renowned Australian soprano has died in Sydney. Born Helen Mitchell, near Melbourne, she took her stage name from the city. Having been trained in Paris, she performed in the world's great opera houses, and such was her reputation that she could command the casting. Among the many roles she made her own were Mimi in *La Bohème*, Gilda in *Rigoletto*, and Desdemona in *Othello*. Like Caruso, with whom she sang, she was among the first opera singers to make recordings. Peach Melba and Melba toast are named in her honor. She was famous for her many "last" performances.

SINO-JAPANESE WAR

Japanese troops attack a Chinese garrison at Mukden, in the northern province of Manchuria, in September and speedily occupy the entire province. The following February, they set up the puppet state of Manchukuo, with the former Chinese Emperor Pu Yi as emperor.

In January of 1932, Japanese troops enter the city of Shanghai, starting an invasion of China. Although the Chinese drive them out of the city in March, the Japanese continue acts of aggression against Chinese territory for the next five years.

LEFT: Invading Japanese forces encounter stiff resistance and, backed by armored vehicles, fire from the safety of a reinforced emplacement.

BELOW: Defending Chinese soldiers return rifle fire from behind a hastily constructed barricade on Paoshan Street.

ABOVE: Japanese soldiers place logs across a river for their tanks to cross.

RIGHT: An armed convoy of Japanese sailors races through the city.

BELOW: General Tsai, commander of the 19th Route Army, observes the damaging effect of one of his howitzers.

THE WEST SINKS INTO DEPRESSION

Depression tightens its grip on the Western world in the continuous fallout from the Wall Street Crash of 1929. In the United States, Franklin D. Roosevelt comes to power on his promise of a New Deal to fight poverty. In Germany, Adolf Hitler's policies are equally attractive to a nation still recovering from World War I. The world of physics concentrates on detail: the development of particle accelerators allows scientists to observe what are, at the time, considered to be the smallest building blocks of the universe. Amelia Earhart becomes the first woman to fly the Atlantic.

1932

Jan	31	Japan captures Shanghai
Mar	2	The infant son of aviator Charles Lindbergh is kidnapped. Sadly, he will be found dead two months later
May	10	President Paul Doumer of France is assassinated
	21	Amelia Earhart flies from Canada to the United Kingdom
July	5	Antonio Salazar becomes dictator of Portugal
Aug	6	First Venice Film Festival
Nov	8	Democrat Franklin D. Roosevelt is elected president of the United States

ABOVE: Mies van der Rohe is director of the Bauhaus (1930–33). The Seagram Building, completed in 1958, epitomizes Bauhaus principles.

LAND FROM THE SEA

The drainage scheme of the Zuider Zee in the Netherlands is completed, vastly increasing the amount of available arable farmland and reducing the risk of flooding from the North Sea.

GRAN CHACO WAR

War breaks out between Bolivia and Paraguay over their disputed border, the Chaco Boreal or Gran Chaco. It is a potential shipping route to the sea for oil. Paraguay declares war, but Bolivia is better trained and equipped, and has success. Paraguay then fully mobilizes and counterattacks. The war drags on until June 1935. Both sides became war-weary and, at a peace treaty in 1938, Paraguay receives the Chaco region and Bolivia gains access to the Atlantic via two rivers.

DE VALERA LEADS IRELAND

Éamon de Valera wins the Irish general election and becomes prime minister the following month. He begins to loosen Irish ties with Britain, adopting a new constitution in 1937, which renames the Irish Free State as Eire.

THE INTERNATIONAL STYLE

This work on architecture, by Philip Johnson and Henry-Russell Hitchcock, publicizes the modernist style and influences a whole generation of architects. The book, together with the arrival of exiled scholars and architects from Nazi Germany, will influence the development of architecture, first in North America, then all over the world. The book describes a style in which form follows function.

FDR FOR PRESIDENT

Franklin D. Roosevelt wins the presidential election by a landslide for the Democrats, defeating the sitting Republican president, Herbert Hoover. Roosevelt, who is in a wheelchair as a result of polio, wins all but six of the 48 states of the Union.

ANDRE LOUIS RENE MAGINOT
(1877–1932)

The French politician André Maginot has died this year. During the 1920s, in preparation for a possible further war with Germany, he organized fortifications around the Franco-German border, known as the Maginot Line. When war came, the Germans invaded through Belgium, rendering these defenses useless. Maginot's name is doomed to go down in history attached to a useless mega-project.

NEUTRON DISCOVERED . . .

English physicist James Chadwick discovers the neutron, a particle with no electrical charge found in the nuclei of all atoms except hydrogen.

. . . AND POSITRON DISCOVERED

U.S. physicist Carl D. Anderson discovers the positron (positive electron), the first subatomic particle of antimatter.

HINDENBURG BEATS HITLER

President Hindenburg wins reelection in the German presidential election in a close-run contest with Adolf Hitler. In the general election in July, the Nazis become the biggest party, although they do not have a majority and so cannot form a government.

PARTICLE ACCELERATOR

Physicists John Cockroft of England and Ernest Walton of Ireland build the first linear atomic particle accelerator. With it, they bombard lithium with protons and transform it into helium. This is the first artificial atomic transformation.

BELOW: Jobless Californians contemplate a bleak future as they wait in line for unemployment compensation.

ABOVE: Amelia Earhart is set to become the first woman to fly solo across the Atlantic. Her route will take her from Harbour Grace, Newfoundland, to Londonderry, Northern Ireland.

BROTHER CAN YOU SPARE A DIME?

This mournful tune, written by E.Y. Harburg and Jay Gorney, is the archetypal song of the Depression. It will later become popular when sung by Bing Crosby and Rudy Vallee.

WOMAN'S ATLANTIC SOLO

American aviator Amelia Earhart (1898–1937) becomes the first woman to fly the Atlantic solo, from Harbour Grace, Newfoundland, to Northern Ireland.

DOUBLE DUTCH

Flemish, a language almost identical to Dutch, becomes the official language of Belgium's Flemish provinces, which border on Holland. French becomes the official language of the Walloon provinces.

BRAVE NEW WORLD

Aldous Huxley's seminal dystopian novel is published. It depicts a society in which humans are "programmed" from birth to accept their social destiny, and are graded in a pseudoscientific caste system, from intellectual to "semi-moron." The novel describes what happens when a savage from a reservation confronts the World Controller and plays out the debate between social stability and individual freedom.

AMERICAN OLYMPICS

In February, worldwide economic depression and warm weather leave competitors and snow thin on the ground at the Third Olympic Winter Games in Lake Placid, New York. Again, the North Americans (who make up half of the competitors) and the Scandinavians dominate. Nineteen year old Sonja Henie of Norway repeats her success in women's figure skating.

In July, Los Angeles hosts the tenth Olympic Games, which are depleted by economic turmoil. Only 1,400 athletes, half the 1928 tally, travel to California. The International Olympic Committee block Olympic hero Paavo Nurmi from adding to his 9 golds and three silvers, for breaking rules on his amateur status. With two golds and a silver, American Mildred "Babe" Didrikson is the star of the games.

LEFT AND BELOW: Los Angeles is home to the Tenth Olympic Games and, despite the world's money worries, thousands attend to cheer the athletes to ever greater feats.

THE NEW DEAL VERSUS NATIONAL SOCIALISM

In Germany, the Reichstag burns, Adolf Hitler takes power, and his secret police, the Gestapo, begin the process of what will become known as ethnic cleansing. In the United States, Roosevelt deals with financial collapse by putting his New Deal into practice. Everyone can celebrate as prohibition ends. The League of Nations, formed after World War I to prevent any future global warfare, disintegrates. Cuba becomes a dictatorship. American aviator Wiley Post flies round the world in just over a week and in the cinema, *King Kong* storms the box office.

1933

Jan	30	Hitler is appointed chancellor of Germany
Feb	27	Reichstag burns down
Mar	5	Roosevelt closes banks for a cooling off period
May	27	Japan leaves the League of Nations
June	23	Hitler dissolves all opposition parties
Oct	14	Germany leaves the League of Nations
Dec	5	Prohibition repealed in the United States

ABOVE: Thomas Mann speaks out against the increasing dangers of political extremism and, after 1933, moves from Germany to Switzerland. He settles in the United States in 1936.

NEW DEAL, NEW ENERGY

Franklin D. Roosevelt takes power in the United States and begins to tackle the economic crisis. New Deal legislation is soon introduced to control industry and production, money is pumped into public works, farmers and banks are bailed out with public money, and a vast scheme is introduced to revive the Tennessee Valley. Three million acres will be restored to cultivation, erosion halted, and 42 dams and eight hydroelectric projects built. The energy of the new government does much to lift depression in the United States.

LEAVING THE LEAGUE

Japan withdraws from the League of Nations in May; Germany follows in October.

ABOVE: Prohibition sees millions of gallons of illegal alcohol go down the drain and an increase in crime. The Eighteenth Amendment that brought it about is repealed in December 1933.

ART DIASPORA

Nazi Germany drives out "degenerate" artists. They include composers Kurt Weill (1900–1950) and Arnold Schoenberg (1874–1951), and writers Thomas Mann (1875–1955) and Bertolt Brecht (1898–1956).

BACK TO MOTHER

The dominion of Newfoundland, which received its independence from Britain in 1917, reverts to colonial status after complete financial collapse.

ABOVE: The Marx Brothers' antiwar satire, *Duck Soup*, stars the hapless team delivering their distinctive brand of irreverence.

DUCK SOUP

The Marx Brothers star in this antiwar satire. Their rapid-fire irreverent humor has a lasting influence on cinema comedy.

THE REICHSTAG BURNS

In February, fire guts the Reichstag, the parliament building in Berlin. A young Dutchman is arrested, but the new Nazi government blames the Communist party. The excuse is used to suspend civil liberties such as freedom of speech and of the press and to crack down on political opponents.

CUBAN DICTATOR

In Cuba, the army, led by Fulgencio Batista and supported by the United States, overthrows President Machado and takes power in a coup in August. Batista becomes increasingly dictatorial, and although he will go into voluntary exile in the Dominican Republic in 1944, he will return to power by another coup in 1952. He will hang onto power until 1959.

PAINLESS CHILDBIRTH

Grantley Dick-Read publishes *Natural Childbirth* in the United States, a manual of exercises and procedures for childbirth without drugs.

POLYTHENE BY CHANCE

British chemists accidentally discover the plastic polythene (polyethylene) while doing experiments on high pressures. Its discovery is based on research by a Dutch chemist, AMJS Michels of Amsterdam. It is the first true plastic made by the polymerization of ethylene.

BELOW: "Tea, anyone?" The all-electric Teasmade is launched in Britain by Goblin.

SOLO WORLD FLIGHT

Pioneer American aviator Wiley Post makes the first solo flight around the world, using a single-engined Lockheed airplane. The flight takes him 7 days, 18 hours, and 49 minutes.

THE BIG BANG

Belgian astronomer and priest Georges Lemaître (1894–1956) publishes *Discussion on the Evolution of the Universe*, which first states the theory of the Big Bang. It is based on his 1927 theory of the cosmic egg, the beginning of all things.

GESTAPO CRACKDOWN

In Germany, the Gestapo begin closing gay institutions, bars, clubs, journals, and libraries, burning magazines and books, and hunting down and imprisoning homosexuals. They dissolve the Bund Deutsches Frauenverein and other women's organizations, remove women from the government and professions, and award "Aryan" women cash for producing children.

CONSERVATION WORK

The Civilian Conservation Corps is founded in the United States to create work, enlisting three million young men for environmental conservation work. They plant more than two billion trees, build small dams, aid wildlife restoration, and tackle soil erosion.

TECHNICAL PROGRESS

The Chicago Exposition portrays technical progress since the city's foundation in 1833. Rocket cars carry millions of visitors along the elevated Skyride. General Motors shows off its fast vehicle assembly line, and soya products are displayed in the Ford Motor Company's Industrialized American Barn.

MONKEY BUSINESS

King Kong, a film directed by Merian Cooper and Ernest Schoedsack, breaks all box office records. It stars Fay Wray, Robert Armstrong, the Empire State Building, and special effects by Willis H. O'Brien.

TUBERCULOSIS SANATORIUM

Finnish architect Alvar Aalto (1889–1976) is the leading modern architect in Scandinavia. His Sanatorium Paimio, Finland, shows how the modernist style adapts well to buildings with a humanitarian purpose. The clean lines and sound planning of the building are praised by Le Corbusier, Mies van der Rohe, and Walter Gropius.

MAN AT THE CROSSROADS

Eminent Mexican muralist Diego Rivera (1886–1957) completes this work for the Rockefeller Center's RCA Building. Because of its content (it includes a portrait of Lenin), the mural is destroyed.

42ND STREET

Busby Berkeley (1895–1976) is the choreographer of the elaborate set pieces in this musical, which immediately becomes a classic. The film was preceded by *Gold Diggers of 1933*. A number of other films follow in which Berkeley is given full rein to include similar set pieces where special effects produce kaleidoscope-like patterns of precision dancers.

MORNING TEA

The Teasmade, the first all-electric automatic teamaker, invented in the U.K. by Brenner Thornton in 1932 and stylishly designed, is marketed by the British company, Goblin.

NOT CRICKET

During the "Bodyline" cricket tour of Australia, the tactics of the English team cause anger and draw diplomatic protests. A number of Australians are hit as England bowls at the bodies of the batsmen in the hope of catches as they fend the ball off or hook it in the air. The most demonic of the demon bowlers is Harold Larwood.

RIGHT: Pretty in polythene, despite the weather.

THE LONG KNIVES AND THE LONG MARCH

Hitler consolidates his position by destroying the enemy within during the Night of the Long Knives. In China, the Long March begins as Chinese Communists, including Mao Zedong, begin their epic walk to escape from Chiang Kai-shek's Nationalist troops. In the Soviet Union, Stalin's purges continue unchecked. In the United States, the first stirrings of black Islam are heard. Tornadoes tear across the Dust Bowl of the Midwest, devastating the already depleted prairies. In Italy, Fascist dictator Mussolini hitches his star to the Italian football team's triumph in the second World Cup.

1934

May	23	Bonnie Parker and Clyde Barrow die in a hail of bullets
June	10	Italy wins football's second World Cup
	30	The Night of the Long Knives among Germany's Nazis
July	2	Lázaro Cárdenas, revolutionary leader, becomes president of Mexico
	25	Chancellor Dollfuss is assassinated in Austria
Sep	26	Liner *Queen Mary* launched
Oct	21	The Long March begins in China

STORMTROOPERS STORMED
German chancellor Hitler crushes the S.A. (Sturmabteilung), known and feared as the Brown Shirts, and kills their leaders in the Night of the Long Knives. The excuse for the killing is that the S.A. were plotting a coup. As a result, Hitler now has complete control over his party. Other opponents of the regime are also killed.

PURGE AND PURGE AGAIN
Stalin begins a massive purge of his opponents following the assassination of the Communist Party leader Sergei Kirov in Leningrad. It is possible that Stalin ordered Kirov's murder himself, but over the next four years more than seven million people are arrested and three million people killed through execution or forced labor. Those killed include more than half the generals in the Red Army, as well as many leading Communist party members.

HEIL HITLER
In Germany, President Hindenburg dies and Hitler takes absolute power, abolishing the presidency and making himself Führer and Reich chancellor. More than 90 percent of voters approve of the action in a referendum held later in the month.

DOLLFUSS ASSASSINATED
Members of the Austrian Nazi Party attempt a coup by killing the chancellor, Engelbert Dollfuss. The unsuccessful coup follows the attempt by the Socialists to seize power in February and further weakens Austrian independence. The Nazis keep up the pressure to unite Austria with Germany.

THE LONG MARCH
Chinese Communists begin the Long March to escape attacks from the Nationalist government. An estimated 100.000 people leave Jiangxi in southern China and march 6.000 miles to safety in Yanan in the northern province of Shaanxi. They will arrive in October 1935.

CONNUBIAL RADIOACTIVITY
French husband and wife physicists Jean-Frédéric and Irène Joliot-Curie discover how to make radioactive elements artificially; they share a Nobel Prize in 1935.

DIONNE QUINTS
Oliva Dionne gives birth to five girls in Callanda, Ontario. Canada's Dionne quints are the first recorded case of quintuplets to be born in one delivery and survive. They are taken away from their parents and raised in a nursery as a public spectacle.

STREAMLINED CARS
Four manufacturers introduce streamlined cars at the International Car Exhibition in Berlin: the models are the Chrysler-Airflow, the Steyr 32 PS, the Tatra 77, and the 1-litre DKW.

ABOVE: Alcatraz prison, on an island in California's San Francisco Bay, opened in 1836 as a military penitentiary and is a state prison from 1934 to 1963.

CAT'S-EYE ROAD STUDS
English road engineer Percy Shaw patents cat's-eye road studs, invented for marking out roads to make them easier to see while driving in fog or at night. They will be in use in 1935.

FORZA ITALIA
Italy triumphs on home soil in the second football World Cup. Thirty two countries take part but Uruguay does not participate. The Italians beat Czechoslovakia 2–1 in the final. This is a great propaganda coup for Mussolini and the Fascists and the Italian team gave the Fascist salute before kick off.

BLACK ISLAM
Black Muslims at the Temple of Islam, a black sect organized in Detroit by Walli Farrad (W.D. Fard), are led by former Baptist teacher Elijah Poole (Elijah Muhammad), Farad's assistant. Until his disappearance in 1934, Poole styles himself the "Messenger of Allah" and advocates black separatism.

DUST DISASTER
Dust storms blow 300 million tons of topsoil from the U.S. Midwest into the Atlantic, damaging some 300 million acres. This is a result of plowing virgin lands when wheat prices were high during World War I.

DIVING FOR GRAVITY

Dutch Professor Felix Andries Vening Meinesz, who has been using submarines to investigate gravity, makes his longest, deepest, and most widely reported dive so far in the submarine K18.

CULTURAL STUDIES

Ruth Benedict, a social anthropologist at Columbia University, publishes *Patterns of Culture*, a groundbreaking work that disseminates the concept of culture. By describing Native American and contemporary European cultures, she helps combat current racist attitudes.

DAWN OF THE PLASTIC AGE

Perspex, a colorful, transparent acrylic plastic, is produced commercially in the U.K. by ICI. The process, discovered in 1930 by ICI chemist Roland Hill, was improved in 1932–1933 by John W.C. Crawford. It incorporates research carried out earlier in the century by German chemists.

COLLECT $200

Monopoly, the game that makes a capitalist of everyone, is launched in the United States. It will be translated to suit the property map of many other countries.

SOMETHING FOR THE WEEKEND

In Britain, Durex manufacture condoms for male contraception. Trojan is a popular U.S. brand.

CHEESE PLEASE

The cheeseburger is the inspiration of a restaurateur in Louisville, Kentucky. He places a slice of cheese on top of grilled meat inside a hamburger bun and lets it soften, before serving it in his restaurant.

THE BACHELORS

French novelist Henri de Montherlant publishes *The Bachelors*, a study of two aging aristocrats. It combines humor with tenderness and comments on a society in which such people no longer fit. Probably his best work, the book is moving because it finds emotional accommodation for the senile and foolish.

WE ROB BANKS

Bonnie Parker and Clyde Barrow, lovers and thieves, die in a hail of machine gun bullets in Louisiana. Their two year crime spree has made them famous and they have become a regular feature in the local media. They will be immortalized by Faye Dunaway and Warren Beatty in Arthur Penn's film *Bonnie and Clyde* (1967).

DUCKS ON FILM

Irascible fowl Donald Duck joins the animated Disney menagerie.

BELOW: Representatives of the German army honor their dead from World War I as they rearm for the next conflict.

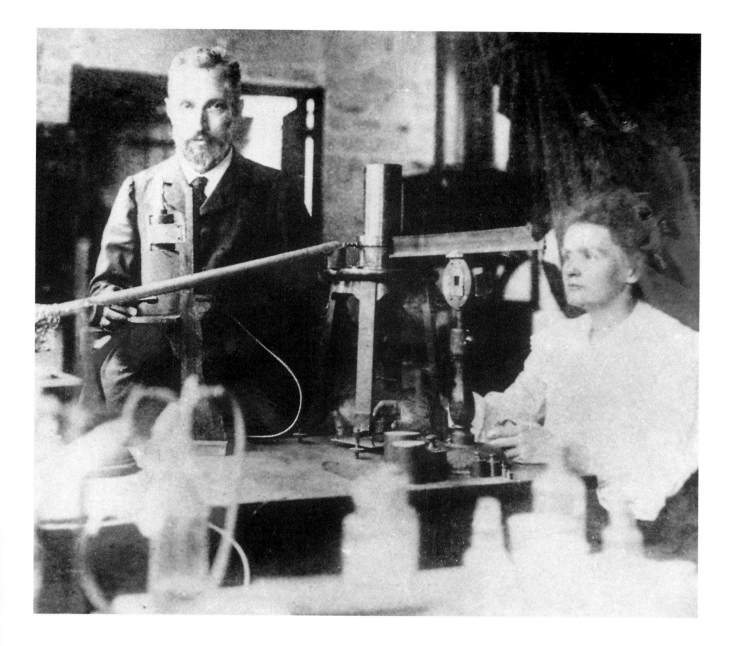

ABOVE: Marie and Pierre Curie work together on the characteristics of magnetism and on radioactivity, a word Marie herself coined in 1898.

DEATH AND THE ARTIST
German graphic artist Käthe Kollwitz begins her series of lithographs (her last such series) that anticipates images from concentration camps. She combines her compassion with self-portraiture.

PENGUIN CLASSIC
Penguins at the London Zoo move into a concrete rookery designed by internationally acclaimed Russian architect Berthold Lubetkin and his London-based group Tecton. One of Britain's best modern buildings, it uses dramatic curving concrete ramps to stunning effect. Not only are they beautiful to look at, but they provide an ideal environment for the pool's inhabitants.

MARIE CURIE
(née MARIA SKLODOWSKA)
(1867–1934)

The Warsaw-born French physicist has died of leukemia, having spent some 40 years working with radioactivity. In Warsaw, she worked as a governess to save the money that would enable her to study physics in Paris. She and her husband, Pierre Curie, were awarded the Nobel Prize for Physics for work on the study of magnetism and radioactivity with Antoine Becquerel in 1903. After Pierre's death, she received the Nobel Prize for Chemistry in 1911 for isolating pure radium. She developed X-radiography during World War I and from 1918 until her death was director of the Radium Institute in Paris.

NAZI SUPREMACY

Adolf Hitler takes power after the German government collapses in January and street warfare breaks out between the Nazis and Communist party members. Apart from Hitler, there are only two Nazis in the 11 member cabinet; the rest are right-wing Nationalists who believe they can curb the excesses of the Nazi Party.

OPPOSITE ABOVE LEFT: Nazism looks to the glorious past when the Knights Templar were the military ideal.

OPPOSITE ABOVE RIGHT: Hitler's desire for a powerful empire is reflected in the legionary-style standards of his troops.

OPPOSITE BELOW: The Nazi ideology is forcefully directed at women and young people as well as the military.

ABOVE: Hitler and his mistress Eva Braun. They will marry in a Berlin bunker on April 29, 1945.

BELOW: Hitler understands the power of public appearances and how crowds behave under a charismatic leader.

GERMANY REARMS AND ITALY GOES TO WAR

War clouds begin to drift over Europe. France and Russia ally in unexpressed apprehension at German expansionism. Hitler makes his intentions clear by creating the German Air Force (Luftwaffe) and reintroducing conscription. He also proves himself to be a master media manipulator with a sound grip on the usefulness of propaganda. Spectacular rallies in Nuremberg, filmed by Leni Riefenstahl, bedazzle the world as anti-Semitism is enshrined in German law. Not to be outdone, Mussolini foments war in Ethiopia. As if anticipating the world-shattering events to come, Charles Richter devises the scale named after him for measuring the force of earthquakes.

1935

Feb	13	Bruno Hauptmann is convicted of killing the Lindbergh's baby	**June**	28	Roosevelt orders the building of Fort Knox
	27	Shirley Temple is the youngest person ever to win an Oscar	**Sep**	8	Alexis Stakhanov, a prodigiously productive Russian coal miner, is established by Stalin as the heroic ideal of the Soviet Worker
Mar	16	Germany introduces conscription			
	21	Persia renames itself Iran		10	U.S. Senator Huey Long dies after being shot two days earlier by Dr. Carl Weiss
Apr	11	Dust storms sweep across the American Midwest			
				15	Hitler introduces laws to exclude German Jews from public life
May	19	T.E. Lawrence dies after a motor-cycling accident five days earlier			
	25	Jesse Owens breaks five world records in one day	**Oct**	2	Italy invades Ethiopia

SAARLAND GOES HOME
Separated from Germany by the Treaty of Versailles, the coal-rich region of Saarland votes overwhelmingly to return to German control.

FRANCE AND RUSSIA ALLY
The U.S.S.R. and France sign a mutual assistance pact pledging assistance if either is attacked. The pact reveals fears in both countries about the intentions of the Nazi government in Germany.

INDIA SCENTS FREEDOM
The British Parliament passes the Government of India Act, which creates a central legislature in Delhi, grants greater self-government to provincial governments, and separates Burma and Aden from India. The Act goes some way to granting India full self-government.

ABOVE: One of the many rallies held by Hitler and the Nazis. The Führer's emotional speeches were heard by thousands of Germans.

INSTITUTIONALIZED ANTI-SEMITISM
Hitler announces new anti-Jewish laws at a mass rally in Nuremberg. Marriage between Jews and non-Jews is banned, and Jews are excluded from working in public services. The new laws are the latest in a long line of anti-Jewish measures in Germany.

GERMANY CALLING UP
Hitler introduces the Luftwaffe (Air Force) and announces that he is reintroducing conscription, and plans an army of 50,000. Both acts make nonsense of the Treaty of Versailles, which was designed to curb German military expansion.

UNIVERSAL TURING MACHINE

British mathematician Alan Turing (1912–1954) devises a theoretical machine, the Universal Turing Machine, for solving mathematical problems. It is never built, but leads to many aspects of modern computers.

PORGY AND BESS

George Gershwin (1898–1927) wanted to create an American opera and this is the result, his last major work. Its use of a black American cast, its tunes, and its ability to close the gap between classical and popular music have kept it in the repertoire ever since.

ONE DAY AT A TIME

Alcoholics Anonymous is founded in New York City by ex-alcoholics Bill Wilson and Dr. Robert Smith as a self-help and support group for alcoholics.

BERG'S VIOLIN CONCERTO

Alban Berg's concerto, famous for combining modern musical techniques (a 12 note row) with quotations from a Lutheran chorale (*Es ist genug*), is finally played in Bach's harmonization at the end of the piece. The work is a memorial to Manon Gropius, who died at the age of 18.

EARTHQUAKE SCALE

U.S. seismologist Charles F. Richter devises a scale, the Richter Scale, for measuring the magnitude of earthquakes. Each number on the scale equals ten times the force of the number below it.

FIRST SUCCESSFUL RADAR

In great secrecy, Scottish physicist Robert Watson-Watt builds the first effective radar equipment for detecting aircraft. He is subsidized by the British government.

NYLON INVENTED

U.S. chemist Wallace H. Carothers, working for the Du Pont Company, invents nylon by polymerizing (making large molecules) of two substances called adipic acid and hexamethylene adipamide. Large scale production will begin in 1938.

WAR BETWEEN ITALY AND ETHIOPIA

Italian forces under Fascist leader Benito Mussolini invade the independent African nation of Ethiopia using aircraft, chemical weapons, and armor. The ill-equipped Ethiopians are forced back and Emperor Haile Selassie flees the capital, Addis Ababa. League of Nations sanctions against Italy are ineffective and Italy eventually leaves the League in 1937. The Italian king is proclaimed emperor of Abyssinia, as the Italians call their new acquisition. Ethiopia remains under Italian control until 1941 when British, French, and Ethiopian forces reinstate the emperor.

THE TRIUMPH OF THE WILL

Shot at the Nuremberg Nazi Party Conference the previous year, this film by Leni Riefenstahl is one of the most effective pieces of Nazi propaganda. She makes it after impressing Hitler with a short film of the previous rally. Her work is a key plank in Hitler's propaganda platform.

FAST WORK

In his car Bluebird, British driver Malcolm Campbell advances the land speed record past the 300 mile per hour barrier. He records a speed of 301.129 miles per hour at the Bonneville Salt Flats in Utah.

FIRST WONDER DRUGS

The first sulphonamide drugs are introduced when German bacteriologist Gerhard Domagk discovers that the red dye prontosil rubra is an active antibacterial agent. Prontosil itself is no longer used.

OPINION POLLS

George Gallup, an Iowa statistician, is asked to gauge reader reaction to newspaper features and founds the American Institute of Public Opinion to carry out market and political research.

BEGINNING OF SOCIAL SECURITY

President Roosevelt signs the Social Security Act into law which will provide benefits for the handicapped, unemployed, and the elderly.

WORKING LIGHT

The Anglepoise lamp, a pivoting desk lamp with a jointed arm designed by a British designer, George Carwardine, is produced in the U.K.

BEER TO GO

Beer in easy-carry, throwaway metal cans is marketed by Kreuger in New Jersey and launched in New York City.

PAYING TO PARK

The first parking meters appear in the streets of Oklahoma City. They were designed and patented in 1932 by the editor of the town's newspaper, Charles Magee.

CAN YOU HEAR ME?

The first wearable hearing aid, with an electric valve and a battery operated amplifier weighing 2.25 pounds is introduced by its British inventor, A. Edwin Stevens. He founds a company named Amplivox to market it.

COLOR PICTURES

The Kodak Company introduces Kodachrome film for taking color transparencies.

ABOVE: An early type of mobile radar detector. Radar, first developed in the U.K., will be an important defensive advantage in World War II.

ALFRED DREYFUS
(c.1859–1935)

The French army officer and subject of a *cause célèbre* has died. Dreyfus, born c.1859 of a Jewish family, was falsely accused of treason in 1893–1894 and sent for life imprisonment to Devil's Island. France was strongly divided over the case and through the active support of many people in political and intellectual life, including the writer Emile Zola and the statesman Clemenceau, he was eventually reinstated in 1906. He went on to fight in World War I and was awarded the Légion d'honneur.

THOMAS EDWARD (T.E.) LAWRENCE
(LAWRENCE OF ARABIA)
(1888–1935)

The author of *Seven Pillars of Wisdom*, Col. T.E. Lawrence (Lawrence of Arabia) has been killed in a motorcycling accident near his home in Dorset. Born in 1888 of Anglo-Irish stock, he encountered the Bedouin people when working on an archaeological dig on the Euphrates as a young man and became a fervent admirer of their character and way of life. He was an Arab guerrilla leader in the Arab struggle against the Turks (1916) and was a delegate at the Paris Peace Conference in 1919. Later, to escape his own fame, he enlisted in the Royal Air Force under the name J.H. Ross.

WAR IN SPAIN AND THE BIRTH OF THE AXIS POWERS

Spain becomes the theater of European war as General Franco, supported by Nazi Germany and Fascist Italy, fights against Republican Spain, which is supported by Communists and Socialists from all over Europe and Russia. In Germany, Jesse Owens, the black American super athlete, confounds Hitler by sweeping the board at the Olympic Games in Berlin. Germany, Italy, and Japan form the Axis Powers. In Britain, the prototype of the Spitfire, the fighter plane that will win the Battle of Britain, makes a test flight. The British Broadcasting Corporation transmits the first television programs.

1936

Feb	**26**	Volkswagen factory opens in Germany
Mar	**7**	German troops march into the Rhineland in defiance of the Treaty of Versailles
July	**19**	Spanish Civil War breaks out
Oct	**13**	In England, unemployed workers march from Jarrow to London in protest at unemployment
Dec	**11**	Edward VIII abdicates the British throne

ABOVE: The British film actor and director Charlie Chaplin charms cinema audiences with his comedic, but endearing, performances.

SPEND, SPEND, SPEND

The British economist John Maynard Keynes (1883–1946) publishes *The General Theory of Employment, Interest, and Money*, which advocates public spending to cure unemployment. Keynesian economic theories become widely accepted within a few years and form the basis of the postwar economic boom.

FALSE DAWN IN SPAIN

The Popular Front of left-wing parties wins the general election in Spain. Manuel Azaña becomes prime minister and restores the 1931 Republican constitution. Anticlerical and antilandlord sentiments explode throughout Spain and churches are attacked and land is seized.

UNEASE OVER GERMANY

German troops occupy the Rhineland, which has been demilitarized since 1919. The move alarms France, but Britain makes no protest.

BRITAIN IN THE MIDDLE IN PALESTINE

A revolt against British rule in Palestine breaks out among the Arab population. Jews are murdered and Jewish property is attacked. The revolt leads to the intervention of the British army, which is attacked by both Arabs and Jews.

BRITAIN AND EGYPT

Britain ends its protectorate over Egypt, with the exception the Suez Canal Zone, entering into an alliance with Egypt which lasts for 20 years.

LIFE MAGAZINE

Life Magazine, one of the first magazines to take photojournalism to new heights, is launched in the United States by Henry Luce. It influences America's understanding of world events in a way previously unknown.

ANYTHING FOR LOVE

King Edward VIII abdicates because he wishes to marry a divorcee, the American Wallis Simpson. He is succeeded by his younger brother, George VI. Edward then goes into exile and marries Wallis in France the following June.

IVAN PETROVICH PAVLOV
(1849–1936)

The Russian physiologist, whose laboratory experiments with dogs established the theory of conditioned reflex or conditioned response applicable to human beings, has died. He won the Nobel Prize for his work in 1904.

ABOVE: A shot by photographer Leni Riefenstahl of a gymnast taken at the 1936 Olympic Games held in Berlin.

GREAT SHADES

Polaroid lens antiglare sunglasses, developed by U.S. physicist Edwin Land, are introduced by Land-Wheelwright Laboratories.

AXIS POWERS LINE UP

The Italian and German governments sign the anti-Communist Axis Pact. Later in the month, Germany will sign the Anti-Comintern Pact with Japan.

MODERN TIMES

This is one of a number of virtually silent feature-length films that Charlie Chaplin (1889–1977) produces with his company United Artists. This example brings his brand of serious clowning (Tramp as Everyman) to bear on a satire of the mechanization of modern life and work. Chaplin is writer, director, producer, and co-stars with Paulette Goddard.

OL' MAN RIVER

Black actor and singer Paul Robeson (1898–1976) plays Joe in the film version of *Show Boat*. He turns this song into a personal signature tune and symbol of a black American artist's success and role as social conscience.

ABOVE: The dirigible *Hindenburg* and a passenger aircraft in the States.

MIGRANT MOTHER

Dorthea Lange (1895-1965), while working for the Farm Security Administration, documents the poverty of the people and the erosion of the land during the Great Depression. Lange's photograph, "Migrant Mother," sticks in the public mind more than any other and helps win support for federal aid.

SAFETY IRON

The first electric hand iron with a thermostat goes on sale in the United States. Electric irons first appeared in 1920, but their temperature could not be controlled.

THE PEOPLE'S PORSCHE

The first prototypes of the Volkswagen "Beetle" are displayed at the Berlin Motor Show, designed by Ferdinand Porsche and praised by Adolf Hitler.

MAXIM GORKY (ALEKSEI MAKSIMOVICH PESHKOV) (1868–1936)

The Russian writer has died. He was a largely self-educated peasant who worked in many lowly occupations and described in his writings the life of peasants and outcasts. He was a valiant supporter of the Russian Revolution and had become a national hero.

FALLINGWATER: THE KAUFMANN HOUSE

Frank Lloyd Wright's most famous house is built over a waterfall at Bear Run, Pennsylvania. It is a daring design, both for the way it seems precariously balanced above the water and for the way it mixes old and new materials (concrete with stone and wood).

MUSIC FOR STRINGS, PERCUSSION, AND CELESTA

One of the major works of Béla Bartók's fruitful period in the 1930s, this piece shows his flair for combining different instrumental colors and for handling rhythm.

SANITARY TOWELS

Kotex sanitary napkins are introduced by Kimberley & Clark Co. of Wisconsin, using a wood-cellulose cotton substitute developed for World War battlefield dressings by German chemist Ernst Mahler. Tampax, Inc. is founded in New Brunswick, New Jersey, to produce cotton tampons.

FIRST PUBLIC TV SERVICE

The first regular public electronic TV service is started in Britain by the British Broadcasting Corporation.

ACHTUNG! SPITFIRE!

The first prototype of the British Spitfire fighter plane, designed by Reginald J. Mitchell, makes its test flight.

FLIGHT FROM HAWAII

The first solo flight by a woman from Hawaii to mainland America is made by Amelia Earhart in 18 hours and 16 minutes.

SUCCESSFUL HELICOPTER

In June, the world's first completely successful helicopter, the Focke-Wulf Fw 61, makes its maiden flight.

DESERT TREASURES

The Swedish explorer Sven Hedin returns at age 80 from a nine year trip to the Gobi Desert to investigate the shifting locations of the Lopnor salt lakes. He has discovered a major Stone Age culture between Manchuria and Sinkiang.

FEDERICO GARCIA LORCA
(1899–1936)

The assassination at Granada (on the instructions of the Civil Governor) of the young Spanish poet and dramatist Federico García Lorca (known as Lorca) is one of the shameful incidents of the Spanish Civil War. His works, such as the poems *Gypsy Ballads* (1928) and *Lament for the Death of a Bullfighter* (1935), and the play *Blood Wedding* (1933), capture the intensity of the Spanish spirit.

BELOW: Frank Lloyd Wright, now 69, displays his genius for blending modernistic design into a natural setting in this house.

SPANISH CIVIL WAR

❖KEY DATES❖

July 20–Sept 27, 1936 SIEGE OF TOLEDO: A Nationalist garrison of 1,300 holds the palace fortress of the Alcázar against 15,000 Republicans in a siege which is broken by two columns of Nationalist troops on September 26.

July 21, 1936 The world's first large-scale airlift begins when German Junkers Ju 52/3m fly 7,350 Nationalist troops from Morocco to Spain.

Nov. 1, 1936–March 31, 1939 SIEGE OF MADRID: A siege by the Nationalists, which includes artillery and air attacks and civil war within the capital, begins when an anti-Communist revolt breaks out.

January 17, 1937 BATTLE OF MALAGA: The city, defended by 40,000 poorly organized militiamen, falls to three Nationalist columns and nine battalions of Italian mechanized infantry. As the Republicans withdraw, they are ground strafed by Italian and German aircraft. They suffer 15,000 casualties.

March 8–17, 1937 BATTLE OF GUADALAJARA: Some 22,000 Nationalist troops with 30,000 Italians attack the Republicans. They fall back, but launch a counterattack backed by Soviet tanks and aircraft. They rout the Italians, killing 2,000, wounding 4,000, and halting the Nationalists.

April 26, 1937 BOMBING OF GUERNICA: German bombers attack Guernica, capital of the Basque region, ostensibly to support Franco. The city is of no strategic importance, but a third of the population are killed. The raid is a piece of psychological warfare and good practice for the Luftwaffe.

Dec 23, 1938–Feb 10, 1939 BATTLE OF BARCELONA: Six Nationalist armies with four Italian divisions attack northwards in December and push the Republicans back towards Barcelona, which was heavily bombed on January 26. A few days later, the Nationalists occupy the city and about half a million Republican troops and dependents cross the border into France.

Civil war breaks out on July 17 as the Nationalist army, led by General Francisco Franco, rises against the Republican government. Led by Britain and France, many nations pledge noninterference in the war, although both Italy and Germany actively support the rebels. An International Brigade of left-wing activists from Europe and America is formed to support the government and sees action in many battles, notably the siege of Madrid, which begins in November and lasts until March 1939. Many new weapons and tactics are tested in Spain by the backers of both sides. The war will officially end on April 1, 1939, with Franco victorious.

ABOVE: Bombardment and mining are used to devastate historic buildings in cities such as Toledo, Barcelona, and Madrid.

BELOW: Horses are used by both sides to carry pack guns over rough terrain and, if killed, to act as barricades for artillery.

ABOVE: Italy and Germany support Franco with men and equipment. The Republicans are aided by the U.S.S.R. and the International Brigade.

ABOVE: As ever, civil war means upheaval, dispossession, and the movement of vast numbers of refugees around the country.

RIGHT: General Francisco Franco, leader of the Nationalist troops and the figurehead of Spanish Fascism. His victory in 1936 will put Spain in his power until his death in 1977.

HITLER'S OLYMPICS

The Eleventh Olympics and the Fourth Winter Olympics are held in Germany. They give Hitler a chance to showcase his ideology and show off Germany's resurgence and the supposed superiority of the Aryan race through a broad propaganda campaign.

The Winter Games are held in Garmisch-Partenkirchen and see the first alpine event, a combined downhill and slalom competition. Sonja Henie retires after winning her third successive figure-skating gold for Norway and Britain scores an upset win in ice hockey.

The Olympics proper take place in Berlin. For the first time a relay of runners, 3,075 in all, bring a torch from Olympia in Greece to light the Olympic flame in Berlin. Despite Nazi hopes, the undisputed star of the games is not a German but Jesse Owens, a black American. Owens takes gold in the 100 meters, 200 meters, 4x100 meters relay, and the long jump. Hitler leaves the stadium rather than present the medals to a black athlete. The most successful female competitor is swimmer Hendrika "Ria" Mastenbroek of Holland. She wins three golds and a silver.

ABOVE LEFT: The Aryan ideal is exemplified by classical statues. These are used to set the tone for the film record of the games made by director Leni Riefenstahl: Hitler's choice to document what he hopes will be an Olympiad to fuel Nazi propaganda.

ABOVE: The games are extremely well-organized and well-equipped with specially built pools and tracks. No expense is spared to show that Hitler's Germany sees itself as a player on the world's stage.

LEFT: A dramatic Leni Riefenstahl shot of a swimmer. Holland dominates the women's swimming events and Japan and the United States share the honors almost equally in the men's events.

ABOVE: Young German female athletes display the body beautiful. Germany takes gold for the discus and javelin events but does not manage to outpace the athletes from the United States on the track.

ABOVE: Riefenstahl's stylized images, such as this discus thrower, are very powerful. In the real world, the United States takes gold and silver in the discus event and Italy takes bronze.

LEFT: Star of the Olympics is the black American athlete Jesse Owens, who confounds Hitler's "Aryan" expectations by winning gold in four events.

ATROCITIES AND DISASTERS, SHOW TRIALS, AND SNOW WHITE

Japan bombs Shanghai in China and Germany bombs Guernica in the Basque region of Spain. Both atrocities shock the world. In the Soviet Union, Stalin continues his horrific show trials, an excuse to eliminate his enemies. In the United States, the Golden Gate Bridge opens California to all comers. But in New Jersey, the airship Hindenburg explodes while trying to land. The principle of photocopying is established, but no one can think of how to apply it. Walt Disney cheers a gloomy world with the first full-length animated cartoon, *Snow White and the Seven Dwarfs*.

1937

Apr	**26**	Guernica is bombed by Germany at the request of Franco
May	**6**	The airship *Hindenburg* explodes on landing
	27	The Golden Gate Bridge opens in San Francisco
Aug	**22**	Japan invades China by attacking Shanghai
Sep	**28**	Hitler and Mussolini stage a joint "Peace Rally" in Berlin

ABOVE: German ground crew help to steady the *Hindenburg*.

46

HINDENBURG DISASTER
On May 6, the German airship Hindenburg is destroyed in a fire while landing at Lakehurst, New Jersey, killing 33 of its 97 occupants. This accident halts worldwide rigid airship development for generations.

FLOATING ON WATER
The first commercial hydrofoil goes into service on the Rhine River in Germany.

JEAN HARLOW
(HARLEAN CARPENTIER)
(1911–1937)

The American film actress Jean Harlow has died of a brain swelling. Although she was only 26, she had already made a name for herself as a witty and talented screen star. Her films include *Hell's Angels* (1930), *Platinum Blonde* (1931), *Dinner at Eight* (1933), and *Libelled Lady* (1936).

ABOVE: On May 6 in Lakehurst, New Jersey, the hydrogen-fueled *Hindenburg* is consumed by fire while docking.

ATROCITY FOR THE BASQUES
In Guernica, Spain, German aircraft bomb the Basque town of Guernica in northern Spain, killing many inhabitants. The German Air Force supports the Nationalist forces across Spain, giving them air superiority. Pablo Picasso's response to the bombing of the Basque city, with its images of suffering, is one of his best-known works. It becomes an emblem of the destructiveness and brutality of Fascism. The work creates a powerful visual language through the combination of elements from surrealism and symbolism.

CONTRACEPTION GAINS ACCEPTANCE
Contraception is endorsed by the American Medical Association's Committee on Birth Control and by Islam's Grand Mufti, who issues a fatwa permitting Muslims to take any measure to avoid conception if both man and woman agree.

ABOVE: Shipping passes under the San Francisco–Oakland Bay Bridge and the new Golden Gate Bridge beyond to reach the Pacific.

MARCHESE GUGLIELMO MARCONI
(1874–1937)

Italian physicist and inventor Guglielmo Marconi, famous for sending the first radio signals across the Atlantic in 1901, has died. His experiments with the newly discovered electromagnetic waves led to the invention of wireless telegraphy. Marconi developed short-wave radio equipment in England, setting up a worldwide radio telegraph network for the British government.

SNOW WHITE AND THE SEVEN DWARFS
Walt Disney's first full-length animated feature film quickly becomes a hit. It paves the way for countless others, both from Disney and from other studios.

SHOW TRIALS
Stalin continues his plan to silence all opposition by putting various opponents "on trial" and shooting them afterwards.

OF MICE AND MEN
John Steinbeck's novel is valued for its sympathetic portrayal of Lennie, the childlike giant who does not know his own strength.

LA GRANDE ILLUSION
This anti-war film, directed by Jean Renoir, son of the impressionist painter Pierre-Auguste Renoir, tells the story of French prisoners of war who plot their escape from a prison camp during World War I. It explores the crosscurrents of values during the war (patriotism versus class ties, for example) and comes out on the side of humanitarianism.

JET ENGINES BUILT
In England, Frank Whittle at last builds his jet aircraft engine which he had patented in 1930. At the same time, German engineers also build one.

LEFT: King George VI and his family pose after his coronation on May 12.

XEROGRAPHY INVENTED

American law student Chester Carlson demonstrates a form of copying which can give unlimited numbers of copies. He calls it "dry copying" or xerography. It does not come into use for many years.

GOLDEN GATE BRIDGE

The Golden Gate Bridge, spanning the entrance to San Francisco Bay, California, is opened. It becomes the world's longest suspension bridge.

RADIO TELESCOPE

The world's first radio telescope is built by a radio amateur, Grote Reber of Illinois, in his back yard; he uses a disc reflector 30 feet across.

CARTS IN THE AISLES

The supermarket cart is introduced by Sylvan N. Goldman, owner of Standard Food Markets in Oklahoma City. It demonstrates the fast evolution of shopping since 1930, when Harry Socoloff opened the first modern supermarket, the King Kullen Grocery in Queens, New York.

JAVA MAN

Parts of the skull of a one million year old hominid are discovered on the island of Java. It is the earliest known evidence of the "missing link" between apes and humans.

CHEAP LIGHT

Energy efficient fluorescent lighting, developed with help from University of Chicago physicist Arthur Holly Compton, is introduced in the United States by GEC & Westinghouse Electric Corporation.

SHAVE IN THE ROUND

Philips, a Dutch company, produces the Philishave electric razor with circular cutting blades.

SMART MACHINES

The first machine that can learn from experience appears when U.S. engineer Thos Ross makes a mechanical mouse that runs on toy train tracks and learns to find its way through mazes.

ERNEST RUTHERFORD, 1ST BARON RUTHERFORD (1871–1937)

The New Zealand-born British physicist has died. His research into and discoveries concerning the structure and behavior of atoms have earned him the title "father of nuclear physics."

❖ UPDATE ❖
ON THE SINO-JAPANESE WAR

Japanese forces begin a full-scale invasion of China, seizing Beijing and bombing Shanghai in August. Firebombs are used to level Shanghai before the Japanese retake the city they first captured in 1932.

In December, the Japanese capture the city of Nanking: two hundred fifty thousand people are killed and many raped. Japanese forces continue to press south and west throughout China.

KRISTALLNACHT AND PEACE IN OUR TIME

Germany violates the Treaty of Versailles and grabs the Sudetenland. Hitler himself leads the invading army. At a peace conference in Munich in September, appeasement buys a year of peace and British prime minister Neville Chamberlain brings back the infamous "piece of paper." *Kristallnacht,* a night of looting and wrecking of Jewish shops by uniformed Nazis, shows Hitler's contempt for world opinion. Ballpoint pens and instant coffee come to the aid of hard-pressed journalists and nylon stockings are on sale.

1938

Jan	6	Sigmund Freud and some of his students leave Vienna to work in London
Mar	12	Germany annexes Austria
June	30	The first *Superman* comic appears
Sep	27	*Queen Elizabeth I* launched
	30	The Munich Peace Agreement is drawn up
Oct	5	Germany occupies Czech Sudetenland
	21	Japan occupies Canton
Nov	10	*Kristallnacht* in Germany; Jewish shops and businesses attacked
Dec	25	Coelacanth is fished up from the deep

ABOVE: German annexation of Austria and the Czech Sudetenland occurs prior to the outbreak of war in 1939.

ANSCHLUSS

German troops enter Austria and unite the country with Germany. The *Anschluss* (unification) between the two countries is forbidden by the Treaty of Versailles and alarms the rest of Europe.

GERMANY TAKES SUDETENLAND

Sudeten Germans living on the border with Germany demand autonomy from Czechoslovakia. They are prompted by Hitler, who uses this as an excuse to increase pressure on the Czech government.

PEACE IN OUR TIME?

At a conference in Munich between Britain, France, Italy, and Germany to end the Sudeten crisis, the four powers agree that Czechoslovakia must give up the Sudetenland to Germany. The following month, German troops occupy the territory while Poland seizes the Teschen region. Eduard Benes resigns as president of Czechoslovakia. In November, Hungary occupies southern Slovakia. Czechoslovakia is now effectively dismembered.

THE SOUND OF BREAKING GLASS

In a night of looting and violence, more than 7,000 Jewish shops are attacked and many Jews beaten up. Hundreds of synagogues are burned down. *Kristallnacht*, or the Night of Broken Glass, marks a major attack on the Jewish community in Germany.

HOOVER BUILDING, PERIVALE

Strong geometric forms and sparing use of striking color and pattern mark Wallis Gilbert's factory for Hoover on the outskirts of London. It is one of the most notable art deco buildings of its time.

WAR OF THE WORLDS

The power of the mass media is brought home dramatically when thousands panic during this broadcast version of H.G. Wells' science fiction novel *War of the Worlds*, which describes what happens when Martians land on earth. The actor Orson Welles, of the Mercury Radio Theatre, reads out the lines that scare so many listeners.

PICTURE POST

One of the most influential picture magazines, *Picture Post*, brings the news and contemporary events to life with pictures and telling captions to Britain as *Life* is doing the same in the United States.

BILLY THE KID

Aaron Copland's music brings the hero to life in *Billy the Kid*, his American folk ballet version of an enduring legend. It is choreographed by Eugene Loring, who also dances the lead role. This is the first of several notable Copland ballet scores based on American folklore.

ABOVE: Orson Welles' radio production of *War of the Worlds* convinces many of his audience that an alien invasion is taking place. His fascination with the power of radio continued throughout his life.

ROCKET DEVELOPMENT

A German team led by engineer Wernher von Braun (1912–1927) builds a liquid fuel rocket that travels about 60 feet, the longest flight to date.

ENTER THE BALLPOINT PEN

Ladislao Biró, a Hungarian journalist, patents the ballpoint pen. It will go into production in 1940, but he makes very little money from it.

SUZANNE LENGLEN
(1899–1938)

The French tennis idol, who was many times a Wimbledon champion, has died. She won her first major championship (women's world hard-court singles in Paris) at the age of 15. She retired in 1927, founded her own tennis school in Paris, and wrote a book on tennis, *Lawn Tennis, the Game of Nations* and a novel, *The Love Game* (both in 1925).

GABRIELE D'ANNUNZIO
(1863–1938)

The Italian writer and patriot, World War I soldier, sailor, and airman, has died. D'Annunzio collaborated with Friedrich Nietzsche on the trilogy *Romances of the Rose* (1889–1894); he became a parliamentary deputy in 1897. Later, colorful achievements include an affair with the actress Eleonora Duse, for whom he wrote plays, and appointing himself dictator of Fiume (Rijeka). He became a supporter of Fascism in later years.

NUCLEAR FISSION DISCOVERED
German radio chemists Otto Hahn and Fritz Strassmann discover nuclear fission by bombarding uranium with neutrons, leading to the development of nuclear power and atomic bombs.

NO MORE BURNT SAUCEPANS
American Du Pont engineer Roy Plunkett accidentally discovers polytetrafluroethylene, a plastic better known as Teflon™ or Fluon™. It is used in astronaut's spacesuits and as a nonstick coating for saucepans.

LIVING FOSSIL
In December, a South African fisherman hauls up a "living fossil," a coelacanth. It is a primitive type of fish that scientists until this time knew only from fossils and believed to have been extinct for 70 million years.

NO MORE DRINKING AND DRIVING
The Drunkometer, the first breathalyzer to test for alcohol in driver's breath, is designed by R.N. Harger. It is tested in Indiana and finds that of 1,750 drivers tested, 250 are drunk.

ABOVE: Nylon stockings bring smiles of sheer delight and prove popular throughout the world.

ENCORA ITALIA
The Italians repeat their World Cup victory in Paris, France, by beating Hungary 4-2 in the final.

MRS. MOODY TAKES WIMBLEDON
American tennis star Helen Wills Moody collects her eighth and final Wimbledon singles crown. With ruthless efficiency, the wins were collected in just nine attempts between 1927 and 1938 and complemented seven US Open titles and six French triumphs.

SAVING THE WHALE
The International Convention for the Regulation of Whaling introduces voluntary quotas for whaling nations, but the Japanese, Russians, and Norwegians ignore the agreement.

ABOVE: A parade through Paris to mark the signing of the Entente Cordiale between France and Britain.

MUSTAFA KEMAL ATATURK
(born MUSTAFA KEMAL)
(1881–1938)

Mustafa Kemal, the Turkish leader later known as Atatürk (Father of the Turks), has died. He was a nationalist leader during and after the World War I. As the first president of modern Turkey in 1923, he was responsible for many reforms, including the emancipation of women and the introduction of the Latin alphabet.

AN AWFUL LOT OF COFFEE

Instant coffee is marketed by Nestlé of Switzerland after a request from the Brazilian government to find a use for Brazil's coffee surpluses. Eight years of research have produced a freeze-dried coffee powder that is reconstituted by adding water.

AIR-CONDITIONED JEWELRY

Tiffany & Co.'s new store on Fifth Avenue, New York City, is the first fully air-conditioned store. Invented by W.H. Carrier in 1902, air conditioning has up to now been used for cooling factories.

VICTORY AND FREEDOM

A "V for Victory" campaign is started by two Belgians working for the BBC in London, who realize that "V" stands for *vrijheid* (freedom) in Flemish and Dutch, and *victoire* (victory) in French. The first Vs appear later on walls in occupied Belgium.

SILK STOCKINGS?

Nylon, invented in the United States by Wallace Hume Carothers, who patented it in 1934, is produced commercially by Du Pont in the United States and used to make women's stockings.

GAS IN CHINA

Lewisite poison gas is used by the Japanese against the Chinese during a series of incursions into China via Manchuria, as well as during amphibious landings to seize parts of the hinterland and major ports.

ABOVE: The Duke of Windsor and Wallis Simpson, for whom he gave up the throne.

BELOW: Street fighting in Manchuria as Japan invades the Chinese mainland.

WAR ENGULFS THE WORLD ONCE MORE

A war-torn decade ends with the greatest conflict of all yet to come. By the end of the year, most of Europe is at war. Allies and Axis Powers line up on opposite sides and America stays out of the fight. On the silver screen, Dorothy and her three eccentric musketeers make a stand against evil in *The Wizard of Oz* and Scarlett O' Hara endures the Civil War on the losing side in *Gone with the Wind*. Meanwhile, scientists are unlocking the secrets of nuclear fission that will lead to the atomic bomb.

1939

Apr	**7**	Italy invades Albania
May	**22**	Germany and Italy form alliance
July	**20**	New Dalai Lama is discovered in Tibet
Aug	**23**	Hitler and Stalin sign the Non-Aggression Pact
Sep	**1**	Germany invades Poland
	3	Germany and England are officially at war
Nov	**8**	Bomb wrecks Munich beer hall where Hitler has been speaking
Dec	**15**	*Gone With The Wind* opens in Atlanta
	18	German pocket battleship, *Graf Spee*, is scuttled by her crew

ABOVE: Polish troops mobilize to face the might of the invading German war machine.

WAR AT LAST

German armies invade Poland from the west, with Russian armies later invading from the east. Britain and France declare war on Germany. British children are evacuated from the cities because of fears of air attacks and the British army lands in France to protect it against a possible German attack. A phony war begins as both sides increase war production, but no fighting takes place.

FRANCO VICTORIOUS

The Spanish Civil War ends with victory for the Nationalist forces of General Franco. Britain and France recognize the new government, which represses all dissent and becomes increasingly Fascist in nature. In April, Spain joins Italy, Germany, and Japan in the Anti-Comintern Pact.

SEPTEMBER 1, 1939

This is English poet Auden's poem mourning for a Europe slipping towards war. It confirms his role as a leading poet of the prewar period and social commentator.

BELOW: The New York Giants and the Brooklyn Dodgers open the 1939 season at Ebbets Field, Brooklyn.

OVERTURES TO WAR

In January, Slovakia declares its independence from Czechoslovakia and becomes a German protectorate. Germany annexes the western Czech provinces of Bohemia and Moravia and the eastern province of Ruthenia is seized by Hungary. Hitler enters Prague in triumph. In the same month, Germany seizes the Baltic region of Memel from Lithuania.

In March, following the German takeover of Czechoslovakia, Hitler denounces the German non-aggression pact with Poland, signed in 1934. He demands the Free City of Danzig, on the Baltic, and routes to eastern Prussia through the Polish corridor, which give Poland access to the sea. Britain and France pledge to defend Poland from attack. In April, they extend this guarantee to Romania and Greece.

In April, the Soviet Union proposes an alliance with Britain and France against Germany and Italy. Britain refuses, but takes urgent steps to rearm; conscription is introduced and arms production is stepped up. France steps up its war effort.

In August, Stalin and German foreign minister Joachim von Ribbentrop sign the Nazi-Soviet Non-Aggression Pact in Moscow, allowing Germany a free hand in western Poland.

ABOVE: German soldiers advance through the rubble-strewn streets of Warsaw.

ITALY EXPANDS
Italy invades and conquers the Adriatic state of Albania, increasing its empire in the Mediterranean.

FINNEGANS WAKE
James Joyce's *Ulysses* had explored the events of a single day; in *Finnegan's Wake*, Joyce turns to the upside-down, inside-out world of night, sleep, and dreams. He creates his own language (involving multi-linguistic wordplay), to write a book which, because of its difficulty, becomes more talked about than read.

EASTER SUNDAY CONCERT
The Daughters of the American Revolution refuse black singer Marian Anderson's request to sing in Constitution Hall, Washington, D.C., because of her race. Eleanor Roosevelt sponsors an outdoor concert at the Lincoln Memorial instead, and around 100,000 people attend.

PHOTOCOMPOSITION
American inventor William C. Hueber introduces the first photocomposition system, replacing metal type.

THE WIZARD OF OZ
The musical film of the novel by L. Frank Baum stars Judy Garland. She wins a special Academy Award for singing "Somewhere over the Rainbow" and is launched on a series of starring roles in major American films.

WILLIAM BUTLER (W.B.) YEATS (1865–1939)

The Irish poet and writer has died at Cap Martin in the Alpes Maritimes, France, his home in recent years. Yeats, who won the Nobel Prize for Literature in 1923, was the author of many collections of verse, including *The Tower* (1928) and *The Winding Stair* (1929), stories and legends such as *The Celtic Twilight* (1893), and plays, including *Cathleen ni Houlihan* (1902). He founded the Irish National Theatre Company at the Abbey Theatre in Dublin.

GONE WITH THE WIND
The film of Margaret Mitchell's novel quickly becomes a worldwide success. Vivien Leigh stars as Scarlett O'Hara and Clark Gable does not give a damn as Rhett Butler.

STAGECOACH
John Ford's classic western stars the "cowboy's cowboy" John "The Duke" Wayne. This is the film that makes Ford's name synonymous with the western and with films looking back on America's past. It is also Wayne's first major role in a big film and it establishes him as a major star.

FIRST JET AIRCRAFT
The German Heinkel He 178, the world's first jet-propelled aircraft, makes its test flight. The engine is designed by Dr. Hans von Ohain. The jet reaches a speed of 313 miles per hour.

SIKORSKY HELICOPTER
Russian-born U.S. engineer Igor Sikorsky designs his first helicopter, the VS-300; it makes a tethered flight in September, but is not suitable for mass production.

SIGMUND FREUD (1856–1939)

The "father of psychoanalysis" has died of cancer in London, having escaped the Nazi regime in his native Austria in 1938. The works of this highly controversial, but profoundly influential proponent of theories of repressed sexuality and the unconscious include *The Interpretation of Dreams* (1900), *The Psychopathology of Everyday Life* (1904), and *Ego and Id* (1923).

NUCLEAR FISSION

Austrian-born physicists Otto Frisch and his aunt Lise Meitner continue the work started by Meitner and Otto Hahn. They realize that the production of barium atoms after the bombardment of uranium nuclei with neutrons means that the nucleus has been split, and call the process "nuclear fission;" this leads to atomic power.

DDT COMES INTO ITS OWN

Swiss chemist Paul Hermann Müller finds that dichlorodiphenyltrichloroethane or DDT, discovered in 1874, is a powerful insecticide. It is successfully tested against the Colorado beetle, a potato pest.

THE HEAT OF THE SUN

The first solar-powered house is built as an experiment at the Massachusetts Institute of Technology. A solar panel on the roof heats water stored in a tank.

AN EARLY ANTIBIOTIC

French scientist René Dubos, working in New York City, discovers the antibiotic tyrothricin, but it proves too poisonous for use on humans.

LITTLE LEAGUE

Carl Stotz and George and Bert Bebble form Little League Baseball in Williamsport, Pennsylvania. The format for youth baseball has since spread across America and the world, and the Little League season now culminates in the Little League World Series between an American team and a foreign side.

THE WORLD'S FAIR

New York's World's Fair focuses on Trylon and Perisphere, a 728 foot high pyramidal tower and a gigantic globe that exhibit futuristic films. Innovative exhibits from 60 nations include a pressure cooker; Electro, a robot who speaks; and Sparks, a toy dog who barks and wags his tail.

ABOVE: On April 26, 1939, Captain Wendel of the German Luftwaffe sets a world air speed record of 468.9 miles per hour.

FINNS WRESTLE WITH THE BEAR

The Soviet Union invades Finland in November, but the attack is thwarted by the Finnish army used to fighting in winter conditions. The Soviet Union has demanded that Finland demilitarize its border defenses and cede islands and a base to the U.S.S.R. Finland has refused and in November the U.S.S.R. sends in an estimated 1 million men against 300,000 Finnish troops. Defending the Mannerheim line and using their skills as ski troops, they inflict heavy losses on the Soviets.

❖KEY DATES❖
IN THE RUSSO-FINNISH WAR

Dec 11, 1939–Jan 8, 1940 SUOMUSSALMI: Two Soviet divisions are annihilated in the woods of eastern Finland in a succession of ambushes and running battles.

Feb 1940 MANNERHEIM LINE: The defenses across the Karelian Isthmus are subject to intense air and artillery bombardment and heavy attacks and in February, despite heavy losses, the Soviet forces break through. This forces the Finns, who had 25,000 killed and 44,000 wounded, to accept Soviet terms. Soviet casualties are estimated at 200,000 dead.

THE POWER OF THE MOVIES

ABOVE LEFT: Barbara Stanwyck, star of many a Hollywood *film noir* and always the most fatale of femmes.

ABOVE: Joan Crawford, undisputed queen of the 1930s genre known as women's pictures.

LEFT: Dashing screen hero Clark Gable will enlist and train as an aerial gunner when the United States enters the war.

ABOVE: Hollywood hoofer Fred Astaire swings a mean shoe on a wartime fundraising tour.

ABOVE: The Hollywood Bond Cavalcade, galaxy of movie stars touring the United States to raise money for War Bonds.

RIGHT: Sound stages at the Warner Brothers Studios in Burbank, California.

RIGHT: A veritable picture palace, the sumptuous interior of the Avalon Theatre in Chicago.

BACKGROUND: The Bay Shore – Sunrise Drive-In Theater, which has room for 1,900 cars.

WINNERS AND ACHIEVERS OF THE 1930s

ACADEMY AWARDS

The Academy of Motion Picture Arts and Sciences was founded in 1927 by the movie industry to honor its artists and craftsmen. All categories of motion picture endeavor are honored, but the most significant are listed below.

BEST ACTOR
1930–31 Lionel Barrymore *A Free Soul*
1931–32 Fredric March *Dr. Jekyll and Mr. Hyde*, Wallace Beery *The Champ (tie)*
1932–33 Charles Laughton *The Private Life of Henry VIII*
1934 Clark Gable *It Happened One Night*
1935 Victor McLaglen *The Informer*
1936 Paul Muni *The Story of Louis Pasteur*
1937 Spencer Tracy *Captains Courageous*
1938 Spencer Tracy *Boys' Town*
1939 Robert Donat *Goodbye, Mr. Chips*

BEST ACTRESS
1930–31 Marie Dressler *Min and Bill*
1931–32 Helen Hayes *The Sin of Madelon Claudet*
1932–33 Katharine Hepburn *Morning Glory*
1934 Claudette Colbert *It Happened One Night*
1935 Bette Davis *Dangerous*
1936 Luise Rainer *The Great Ziegfeld*
1937 Luise Rainer *The Good Earth*
1938 Bette Davis *Jezebel*
1939 Vivien Leigh *Gone with the Wind*

BEST DIRECTOR
1930–31 Norman Taurog *Skippy*
1931–32 Frank Borzage *Bad Girl*
1932–33 Frank Lloyd *Cavalcade*
1934 Frank Capra *It Happened One Night*
1935 John Ford *The Informer*
1936 Frank Capra *Mr Deeds Goes to Town*
1937 Leo McCarey *The Awful Truth*
1938 Frank Capra *You Can't Take It with You*
1939 Victor Fleming *Gone with the Wind*

BEST PICTURE
1930–31 *Cimarron*
1931–32 *Grand Hotel*
1932–33 *Cavalcade*
1934 *It Happened One Night*
1935 *Mutiny on the Bounty*
1936 *The Great Ziegfeld*
1937 *The Life of Emile Zola*
1938 *You Can't Take It with You*
1939 *Gone with the Wind*

NOBEL PRIZES

The Nobel Prizes are an international award granted in the fields of literature, physics, chemistry, physiology or medicine, and peace. The first prizes were awarded in 1901 and funded by the money left in the will of the Swedish inventor, Alfred Nobel (1833–1896), who gave the world dynamite.

PRIZES FOR LITERATURE
1930 Sinclair Lewis (American) for fiction
1931 Erik Axel Karlfeldt (Swedish) for lyric poetry
1932 John Galsworthy (British) for fiction and drama
1933 Ivan Bunin (Soviet) for fiction, short stories and poetry
1934 Luigi Pirandello (Italian) for drama
1935 *No award*
1936 Eugene O'Neill (American) for drama
1937 Roger Martin du Gard (French) for fiction
1938 Pearl S. Buck (American) for fiction
1939 Frans Eemil Sillanpaa (Finnish) for fiction

PRIZES FOR PEACE
1930 Nathan Soderblom (Swedish) for writing on and working for peace
1931 Jane Addams (American) for work with the Women's International League for Peace and Freedom, and Nicholas M. Butler (American) for work with the Carnegie Endowment for International Peace
1932 *No award*
1933 Norman Angell (British) for work with the Royal Institute of International Affairs, the League of Nations, and the National Peace Council

1934 Arthur Henderson (British) for work as president of the World Disarmament Conference
1935 Carl von Ossietzky (German) for promoting world disarmament (award delayed until 1936)
1936 Carlos Saavedra Lamas (Argentine) for negotiating a peace settlement between Bolivia and Paraguay in the Chaco War
1937 Edgar Algernon Robert Gascoyne Cecil (British) for promoting the League of Nations and working with peace movements
1938 The International Office for Refugees for directing relief work among refugees
1939 *No award*

PRIZES FOR PHYSICS
1930 Sir Chandrasekhara Venkata Raman (Indian) for discovering a new effect in radiation from elements
1931 *No award*
1932 Werner Heisenberg (German) for founding quantum mechanics, which led to discoveries in hydrogen
1933 Paul Dirac (British) and Erwin Schrödinger (Austrian) for discovering new forms of atomic theory
1934 *No award*
1935 Sir James Chadwick (British) for discovering the neutron
1936 Carl David Anderson (American) for discovering the positron, and Victor Hess (Austrian) for cosmic rays
1937 Clinton Davisson (American) and George Thomson (British) for discovering the diffraction of electrons by crystals
1938 Enrico Fermi (Italian) for discovering new radioactive elements beyond uranium
1939 Ernest Lawrence (American) for inventing the cyclotron and working on artificial radioactivity

PRIZES FOR CHEMISTRY
1930 Hans Fischer (German) for studying the coloring matter of blood and leaves and synthesizing hemin
1931 Carl Bosch and Friedrich Bergius (German) for inventing high-pressure methods of manufacturing ammonia and liquefying coal

1932 Irving Langmuir (American) for discoveries about molecular films absorbed on surfaces
1933 *No award*
1934 Harold Clayton Urey (American) for discovering deuterium (heavy hydrogen)
1935 Frederic and Irene Joliot-Curie (French) for synthesizing new radioactive elements
1936 Peter Debye (Dutch) for studies on molecules, dipole moments, electron diffraction and X-rays in gases.
1937 Walter Hayworth (British) for research on carbohydrates and vitamin C, and Paul Karrer (Swiss) for studying carotenoids, flavins and vitamins A and B-2
1938 Richard Kuhn (German) for work on carotenoids and vitamins (declined)
1939 Adolph Butenandt (German) for studying sex hormones (declined), and Leopold Ruzicka (Swiss) for work on polymethylenes

PRIZES FOR PHYSIOLOGY OR MEDICINE
1930 Karl Landsteiner (American) for identifying the four main human blood types
1931 Otto Warburg (German) for discovering that enzymes aid in respiration by tissues
1932 Edgar Adrian and Sir Charles Sherrington (British) for discoveries on the function of neurons
1933 Thomas Morgan (American) for studying the function of chromosomes in heredity
1934 George Minot, William Murphy and George Whipple (American) for discoveries on liver treatment for anemia
1935 Hans Spemann (German) for discovering the organizer-effect in the growth on an embryo
1936 Sir Henry Dale (British) and Otto Loewi (Austrian) for discoveries on the chemical transmission of nerve impulses
1937 Albert Szent-Gyorgyi (Hungarian) for work on oxidation in tissues, vitamin C and fumaric acid
1938 Corneille Heymans (Belgian) for discoveries concerning the regulation of respiration
1939 Gerhard Domagk (German) for discovering Prontosil, the first sulpha drug (declined)

Franklin Delano Roosevelt, President of the United States from 1933 to 1945.

U.S. PRESIDENTS
1929–1933 President Herbert Clark Hoover, *Republican*
1929–1933 Vice President Charles Curtis
1933–1945 President Franklin Delano Roosevelt, *Democrat*
1933–1941 Vice President John N. Garner;
1941–1945 Vice President Henry A. Wallace;
1945 Vice President Harry S. Truman

SITES OF THE OLYMPIC GAMES
1932 SUMMER Los Angeles, California
WINTER Lake Placid, New York
1936 SUMMER Berlin, Germany
WINTER Garmisch-Partenkirchen, Germany

WORLD CUP FINAL MATCHES
YEAR	LOCATION
1930	**Montevideo**

Uruguay defeats Argentina 4-2
| **1934** | **Rome** |

Italy defeats Czechoslovakia 2-1
| **1938** | **Paris** |

Italy defeats Hungary 4-2

INDIANAPOLIS 500
1930 Billy Arnold
1931 Louis Schneider
1932 Fred Frame
1933 Louis Meyer
1934 Bill Cummings
1935 Kelly Petillo
1936 Louis Meyer
1937 Wilbur Shaw
1938 Floyd Roberts
1939 Wilbur Shaw

KENTUCKY DERBY
1930 Gallant Fox
1931 Twenty Grand
1932 Burgoo King

1933 Brokers Tip
1934 Cavalcade
1935 Omaha
1936 Bold Venture
1937 War Admiral
1938 Lawrin
1939 Johnstown

WIMBLEDON CHAMPIONS
1930 MEN Bill Tilden
WOMEN Helen Wills Moody
1931 MEN Sidney B. Wood, Jr.
WOMEN CILLY AUSSEM
1932 MEN Ellsworth Vines
WOMEN Helen Wills Moody
1933 MEN Jack Crawford
WOMEN Helen Wills Moody
1934 MEN Fred Perry
WOMEN Dorothy Round
1935 MEN Fred Perry
WOMEN Helen Wills Moody
1936 MEN Fred Perry
WOMEN Helen Jacobs
1937 MEN Don Budge
WOMEN Dorothy Round

1938 MEN Don Budge
WOMEN Helen Wills Moody
1939 MEN Bobby Riggs
WOMEN Alice Marble

WORLD SERIES CHAMPIONS
1930 Philadelphia Athletics defeat St. Louis Cardinals
1931 St. Louis Cardinals defeat Philadelphia Athletics
1932 New York Yankees defeat Chicago Cubs
1933 New York Giants defeat Washington Senators
1934 St. Louis Cardinals defeat Detroit Tigers
1935 Detroit Tigers defeat Chicago Cubs
1936 New York Yankees defeat New York Giants
1937 New York Yankees defeat New York Giants
1938 New York Yankees defeat Chicago Cubs
1939 New York Yankees defeat Cincinnati Reds